Cat Love Letters

Cat Love Letters

Collected Correspondence of Cats in Love

Leigh W. Rutledge

Paintings by
Robert Crawford

A Dutton Book

DUTTON
Published by the Penguin Group
Penguin Books USA Inc., 375 Hudson Street,
New York, New York 10014, U.S.A.
Penguin Books Ltd, 27 Wrights Lane,
London W8 5TZ, England
Penguin Books Australia Ltd, Ringwood,
Victoria, Australia
Penguin Books Canada Ltd, 10 Alcorn Avenue,
Toronto, Ontario, Canada M4V 3B2
Penguin Books (N.Z.) Ltd, 182–190 Wairau Road,
Auckland 10, New Zealand

Penguin Books Ltd, Registered Offices:
Harmondsworth, Middlesex, England

First published by Dutton, an imprint of Dutton Signet, a division of Penguin Books USA Inc.
Distributed in Canada by McClelland & Stewart Inc.

First Printing, February, 1994
1 3 5 7 9 10 8 6 4 2

REGISTERED TRADEMARK— MARCA REGISTRADA

LIBRARY OF CONGRESS CATALOGING IN PUBLICATION DATA:
Rutledge, Leigh W.
    Cat love letters / Leigh W. Rutledge.
        p.   cm.
    ISBN 0-525-93757-9
    1. Cats— Humor. 2. Love letters— Humor. I. Title.
PN6231.C23R86 1994   93-2528
818' .5402— dc20   CIP

Printed in the United States of America
Designed by Inkstone

For Charlotte

Tonya
and
Peach

Confession

Dear Mr. Peach,

I have something ridiculous to tell you. I should have told you this evening when I saw you chasing moths across the lawn, but I held my tongue and am now foolishly writing instead. You will say to yourself, "Here is another poor cat in heat trying to throw herself at me." You will hiss in my face, you will chase me from your garden. You will say, "Here is a stupid creature, barely more than a kitten, and she is carried away by the spring weather." I am in love with you. I have been since the first day you moved into the house next door. I thought maybe we could become friends. But that special feeling in my whiskers—do tomcats get it, also?—has let me know that friendship is not enough. Now, whether I'm lying by my kitty dish and contemplating my milk, or sitting in the window and watching butterflies, you are all I think of. I should have kept my silence, but every time I see you I suffer from a want of strength. Tomorrow all my inhibitions will return, and I'll think myself crazed for having written you at all. No reply is necessary from you now. In fact, I'd rather you didn't answer at all, for fear of what your response might be. For now, I'm content to worship you from afar. Foolishly. Deliriously. With both ears quivering.

Yours most sincerely,
Miss Gabbeldoff

My dearest Tonya,

Do you think I hadn't noticed? You must think me a callous and worldly cat. Oh, what a sweet and ingenuous kit- ten you are! I may not have felt it in my whiskers (no, tom- cats are different in many ways, as I hope to teach you), but couldn't you sense my friskiness, barely contained, as I played in the front yard tonight? I saw you first among the geraniums this afternoon and thought: "Will she come over? Or will she chase bugs by herself?" Yes, yes—my tail can barely contain itself. Meet me by the birdbath at midnight.

Yours—all yours,
Peaches

The birdbath at midnight! I am <u>mad</u> with happiness. I can't stop purring—and yet there are no hands petting me! Of course I'll be there! Deranged dogcatchers couldn't keep me away! I never knew such joy was possible!

My whiskers are still trembling, my tail and claws are on fire! That beautiful birdbath! I can never look at it in the same way again! At first, I was worried you wouldn't show up. Then, when you did, I worried the neighbors would hear us and throw shoes at us. But then, as if under a spell, I didn't care. Let them hear us howl! Let them hear our love! I cherish the marks on the back of my neck where you pulled all the fur out with your teeth! All day today I have lolled among the sofa pillows and thought: "He really <u>does</u> care for me." I didn't even want to lick myself for fear of washing away your smell! You're right—tomcats are different. What a wonderful difference! Oh, tell me this cloudless heaven isn't a dream.

Your adoring
Tonya

It is a dream. Perfect. Idyllic. When you started to lick my ears, I thought, "There is still happiness in life for a cat like me." When—yowling and pawing the ground—you finally offered yourself to me, I thought, "There are still miracles." I had resigned myself to the cautious and predictable life of an aging house cat. Since last night I haven't spent a moment without adoring you, without wanting you again and again and again. Meet me tonight by the birdbath once more.

Where are you? It has now been three days since I last heard from you. Why have you abandoned me? What have I done to deserve this? Every day I go out, and you aren't in the geraniums, you aren't by the birdbath, you aren't up in the maple tree. I push aside the curtains with my nose and peek through the window every hour to catch some glimpse of you, but you <u>aren't there</u>. Did I say something wrong? Did I <u>do</u> something wrong? Don't let me suffer in silence like this. <u>WHERE ARE YOU?!</u>

My beloved,

I had no warning. I was taken to the vet's to get my shots—and they left me there for the weekend while they went to the beach. One moment I was sleeping in the window, dreaming only of you—the next I was being dragged away from my home in a cardboard box. What panic! What misery! I sat in a cage at the vet's for three days, with some howling Siamese on one side of me and a whimpering puppy on the other; only my thoughts of you kept me from going mad! Oh, my beloved—teach me again how tomcats are different! I have to see you. Tonight. Meet me among the dahlias by the back porch. I count the hours.

Your Tonya

Do you still love me? Or have you found another eager kitten to take my place while I was gone?

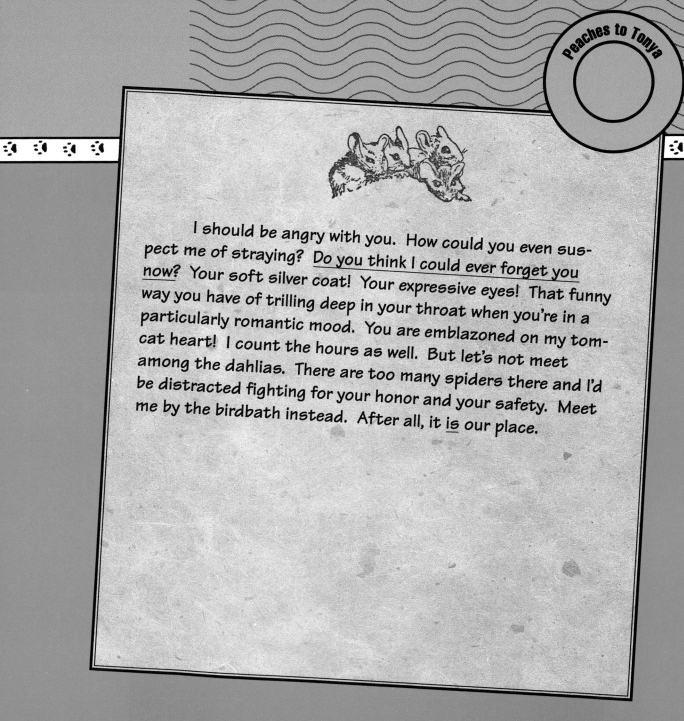

I should be angry with you. How could you even suspect me of straying? <u>Do you think I could ever forget you now?</u> Your soft silver coat! Your expressive eyes! That funny way you have of trilling deep in your throat when you're in a particularly romantic mood. You are emblazoned on my tom-cat heart! I count the hours as well. But let's not meet among the dahlias. There are too many spiders there and I'd be distracted fighting for your honor and your safety. Meet me by the birdbath instead. After all, it <u>is</u> our place.

I love you, I love you, I love you, I love you, I love you! You make me feel as if I've been rolling in a field of catnip! I shall never be able to look at any birdbath the same way ever again!

So you decided not to come last night. What is your excuse now? They wouldn't let you out? You dozed off on top of the television and woke up too late? You were inadvertently shut in one of the closets? What kind of feeble alibi am I going to hear? I've seen the way that hot little black cat looks at you from across the street. What do they call her? Spitfire? Well, tell that slick little minx to keep her paws off you. She thinks that just because she's part Persian she's entitled to anything she wants. I happen to know that her grandmother was a mangy old half-breed who slept with every alley cat in the neighborhood. Is that what you want? Do I now have to paint my claws fuchsia and put colored bows in my hair to keep you interested? I await your reply.

Really you are too silly. Your letter made me sick at heart. What happened to the eager young kitten who once thought I could do no wrong? Yes, I dozed off. I am older than you are, and I have neither your energy nor your stamina—I certainly don't have your energy for recrimination. What can I do to convince you that my whiskers still belong to you? That my tail, paws, ears, and nose belong only to you? How can I convince you that contentment means sitting with you among the marigolds, your soft paws barely touching mine? Who is this strange black creature across the street? Why do you rant about her? I don't even know who she is. I certainly don't love her. Why do you want to tarnish our precious moments together with such nonsense? Let's never speak of these things again.

My darling—

I'm sorry I swatted you so hard last night. It was just an involuntary reflex. But really, your claws were in too deep. I don't know what's been wrong between us lately. I can't help wondering if there's something deep in both of us that rebels against too close an intimacy, that defies fidelity and romance. My feline brain is at war with itself: my love for you on the one paw, and yet some dark, impenetrable instinct on the other. An instinct that seems to say to me: Our kind will always be alone, separate, solitary. I cannot come to the birdbath tonight! I need time to think—time to "study the walls," as they say. Perhaps in a few days we can get together again. Please try to understand. I just need to sort things out.

Tonya

It's easy for you to speak of time—you're still barely more than a kitten. I'm eight years old, my life is more than half over. These have been the six most glorious weeks of my life! I no longer waste my days dozing on the dining room table, or staring into space dreaming of plump mice. I've discovered a new zest for living—for smelling the flowers, for clawing the sofa, for unraveling the toilet paper! The other night I found myself racing around the house, scurrying from room to room, for no reason at all! I stopped and wondered: "What's come over me? I'm not a kitten anymore." We have fifteen, maybe twenty years at the very most in this life. Who has time to stew and debate and hesitate and worry? Perhaps when you're older, you'll realize that time is the most precious commodity we have. Please, _please_ come to the birdbath tonight—if nothing else as a sign of good faith, of _wanting_ to resolve our differences. If you like, we can just walk in the moonlight or stroll through the chrysanthemums. We can sit in the ivy—we don't even have to say anything. But _meet me._ I'll be there at midnight, waiting for you.

I suppose then that I must interpret this as your final answer. I waited for two hours. After the first fifteen minutes, my tomcat heart sank in misery—I knew you weren't coming. But I stayed and waited in the moonlight, watching the clouds roll across the sky, and remembered that first wonderful night by the birdbath, and then that other night just a few weeks ago when you brought me the fat grasshopper, and then the time when we chased each other around the irises and up and down the grass until dawn. My darling, my angelic Tonya—whatever happens, even if you choose never to speak to me again, I shall always love you and cherish the memory of this summer. Remember that you changed a tomcat's life forever. Carry that with you always. No matter what, we'll always have the birdbath.

Your adoring
Mr. Peach

My dear Mr. Peach,

I don't know why anything happens the way it does in this life, especially to cats. I treated you cruelly, I've been the cattiest of kittens. You probably hate me—I wouldn't blame you if you did. I saw you recently from my living room window—there you were, on the grass, your pale fur luminous in the sunlight. I watched you eating grass, I watched you scamper after bugs—and I saw you looking up in the trees and over into our yard, and I knew you were looking for me. It pierced my heart. What can I say to you, you who showed me how to track beetles in the moonlight, you who showed me ways to derive pleasure from whiskers that I never dreamed were possible? The truth is that passion sometimes dies. It will seem like a weak explanation, but there it is. You told me once that I'd changed your life forever. I must tell you now that you have changed mine. You showed me things in the garden—in the world!—that I'd never even imagined were there. Please believe me when I tell you I will always have the deepest affection for you, even if the nature of our friendship has inevitably changed. I will always cherish the memory of this summer as the season of my first love. It was wonderful beyond words.

Your friend,
Tonya Gabbeldoff

To: Mr. Beardsley S. Furr
From: Mr. Peaches L. Keen

My Dear Old Friend,

After so long a silence, the devastation of heartbreaking news. I have just received word that Tonya is dead. She was hit by a car while playing with a leaf that was blowing in the road. The driver, of course, did not even stop. They found her in the gutter; she wasn't killed at first, but was trying to crawl home. She didn't make it.

A friend was kind enough to notify me of her death. As you know, she and her family moved from here two years ago. Tonya and I never really spoke again after the end of our affair. She avoided me, and I didn't press the issue with her. I never even completely understood why the affair ended—it just did. (Kittens are so cavalier about love, aren't they? But then, I suppose they can afford to be. Remember what heartless creatures we once were?) When she moved, I wanted desperately to go and say good-bye. But my pride wouldn't let me. The sight of the moving van disappearing down the street left me heartbroken. I felt in that moment like the most foolish cat who has ever lived. Of course now there will be no reconciliation, no reunion. I knew there wouldn't be, but my heart always ached for it—impractically, stupidly.

I am very much an old cat now. I spend my days lying in the grass (when I go out at all), too tired even to lift a paw and swat at the flies that pass by or land on my nose. I am content in my own way, although the days seem to evaporate, one after the other, like drops of summer rain on warm pavement. I spend too much time remembering <u>her</u>. I still dream of her almost every day.

Oh, Beardsley, why is life so cruel? Why should a birdbath be indestructible and live forever, while Tonya had only a handful of years on this earth? If only you could have seen her! She was the most winsome kitten I'd ever known. No cat, no human, no god could have resisted her! She was like a fleeting light across a sea of darkness. And I shall never forget her. But then, I couldn't, even if I wanted to.

My best to you and your darling Greta.

Your friend,
Mr. Peach

❖ Miss T. Luft ❖

To: Mr. Peaches L. Keen
From: Miss Tomasina Luft

Dear Mr. Peaches:

When I was cleaning out Tonya's belongings yesterday, I came across the enclosed envelope with your name on it. (Please excuse the dust, but it was in an old box of her favorite things.) I have no idea what it means exactly, but I thought you would probably know and would like to have it. Tonya spoke of you often, I know she was very fond of you.

Sincerely,
Miss Tomasina Luft

Mr. Peach ♡

Snowball
and
Spitfire

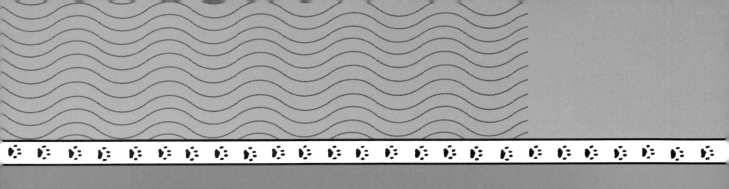

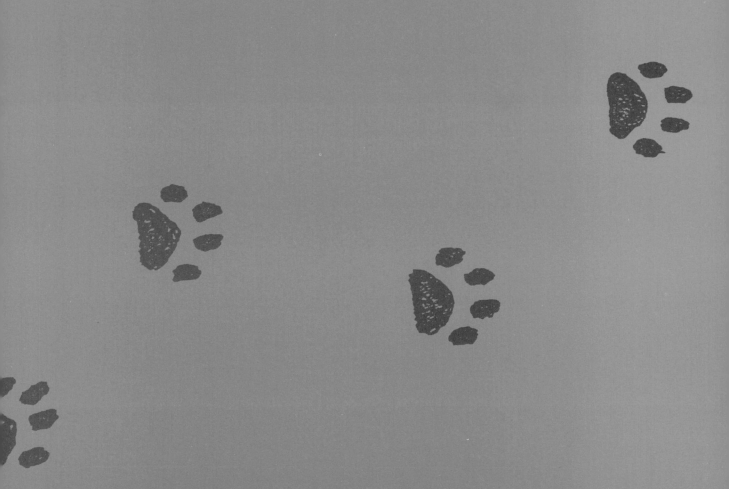

My dear Miss Spitfire,

I hope you don't think me presumptuous, but you can hardly fail to have noticed that I've been admiring you for some weeks now. In fact, is it my imagination or have you been purposely strolling back and forth in front of my house the last few days? (With your tail stuck straight up in the air, no less, it seems to me!) I certainly would enjoy getting to know you better. I mean to say, I'd really <u>love</u> the opportunity to get together with you sometime. You are, I'm sure you've heard a hundred times before, a singularly <u>spicy</u> little creature. And once we got together, I think you'd find that I'm a pretty interesting cat myself. Please, won't you let me pay you a visit sometime? I'd really like to. It would mean a lot to me. I know you must get a dozen letters like this every day, but tell me when we can meet, and I'll certainly be there.

—Snowball

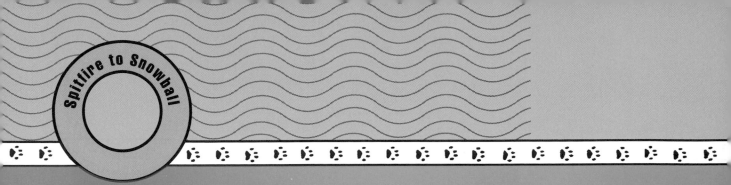

Spittire to Snowball

What do you have to offer?

I saw you today rummaging through the Browns' trash can and it was all I could do to restrain myself. I'm sure I could satisfy you. Please, say yes. Just one quick meeting. I know you've been with all sorts of tomcats, and if I do say so myself, I think I compare favorably with many of them. Please, _please_, say yes. If it's tuna fish you want, I have _lots_ of tuna fish. I have a little green plastic ball with a bell in it, if that would please you. Name it. Anything. Only, I must see you. Just for a few moments. I promise you won't regret it. My dear, I am absolutely _infatuated_ with you. I know there have been others. I don't care. I even have a lovely little rhinestone collar I could give you. Well, I mean, I don't exactly _have_ it—but I know how to get my paws on it. Please, _please_ say yes.

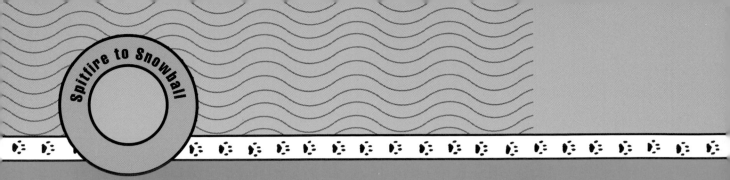

Do you have any catnip?

Snowball to Spitfire

Oh yes, catnip! I have lots of catnip! Is that what you'd like? Is that what pleases you? Certainly. I can get you all the catnip you like! They keep it in a cabinet over the toaster oven. They don't think I know how to get into the cabinet, but I do. I'm a pretty smart cat when it comes right down to it. Oh yes, lots and lots of catnip! It'd be my honor, my _pleasure_ to give you some. Only please, _please_ say yes to me. You are driving me crazy! You are the most voluptuous, _desirable_ little thing I've ever seen in my life. Would you like me to send some catnip over now, or should I wait until we get together?

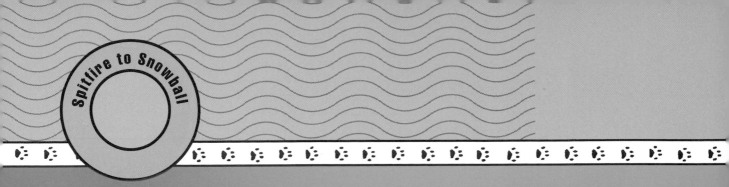

Now. Just the catnip.

My dearest one, it's been two days since I sent you the catnip. You may also have noticed that this morning I dropped the little rhinestone collar on your doorstep. I couldn't help thinking how <u>beautiful</u> it would look on you. I don't mind telling you what a lot of trouble I went through to get it. Not that I'm complaining! No, no—it was an honor to get it for you! I hope you'll remember to wear it when we finally get together. We <u>are</u> getting together, aren't we? <u>Please</u> write me. Some <u>small</u> note of reassurance. Just one or two words. In fact, just one tiny word—"Yes!"—would make me the happiest cat alive. Do you know that last night I could actually smell you on the evening breeze? I was practically hanging from the window screens yowling. Can't you <u>see</u> the effect you have on me? Just five minutes. That's all I ask. It isn't so much, is it?

P.S. You never said whether or not you wanted the little green plastic ball with the bell in it.

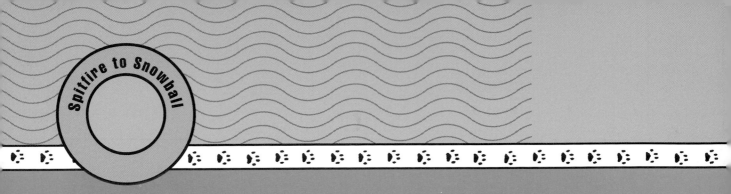

Spitfire to Snowball

Send the ball.

You just can't keep leaving me in limbo like this. Do you know what I'm going through? I sent the catnip. I gave you the collar. I sent the ball over to you four days ago. What more do you want? Isn't it time now that you gave me those five minutes I've asked for? I see you every night. In the alleys. In the lilac bushes. Under parked cars. I'm not objecting. I'm not sitting in judgment. You're beautiful—and Lord knows, we all need to use every advantage we can in this world. I know there are others. I told you I don't mind. Do you think I care one whit about all the stories I've heard? All I know is that I must have you. I've been patient. I've been generous. Now I must insist. I'm certainly as good-looking as many of the other tomcats I've seen you with. Please now, after all this time, tell me what I long to hear. When? And where?

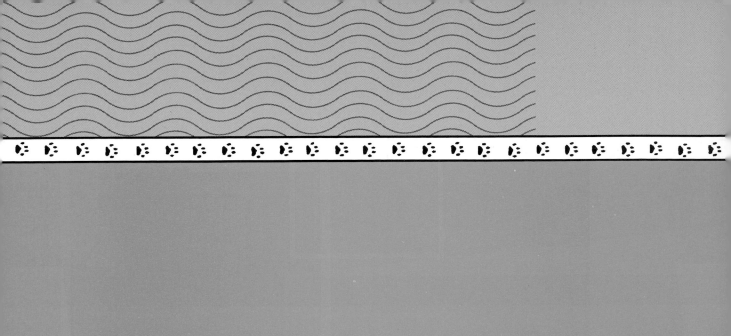

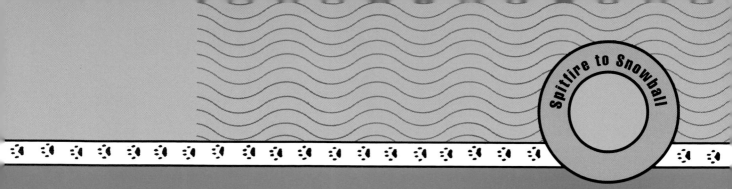

Miss Spitfire regrets to inform you that she is very busy these days and could not possibly see you. (However, if you have any more catnip, feel free to drop it by. Just please don't make any noise—I sleep during the day.)

Shasta
and
J.B.White
Socks

Mr. J.B. White Socks to Hackensack Small Animal Clinic

J.B. WHITE SOCKS

To Whom It May Concern:

I am writing in regards to a tortoiseshell female cat named Shasta who may have been treated at your clinic sometime last year. According to my previous correspondence with the office manager of the Nashville, Tennessee, Humane Shelter, this cat belonged to a woman in Nashville who subsequently moved to Hackensack. The cat is about 1' 2" tall, weighs approximately twelve pounds, has the most beautiful green eyes specked with amber that you've ever seen, is nearly four years old, and has a meow that calls to mind the angels singing in Heaven. It is imperative that I locate this cat as soon as possible. Thank you for your time.

Sincerely,
Mr. J. B. White Socks

P.S. My intentions are strictly honorable.

Hackensack Small Animal Clinic

2828 Squirrel Rump Road / Hackensack, New Jersey 12913

August 3rd

Dear Mr. Socks:

The cat you referred to may have been seen by a veterinarian in this office between February and March of last year. We think the animal's owner later moved to San Diego. Try San Diego. San Diego is definitely the place to look. Best of luck.

Betty O'Donnell
Office Manager

"Caring People Caring for Animals"
Dr. Tom Bird DVM and Dr. Elizabeth Vutz DVM

!p Wanted

istant Wanted
rt time,some
ends. Know-
e of comput-
s, but willing
sharp grad.
sume to P.O.
23756490

s Person for
dies fashion
re, in town.
prox. 40 hrs.
ly in person,
42 West St.

hild Care ,Day
are. Part time
ust love kid &

Personals Advertising

Automobi

1992 Ford T
Auto , A.C. F
Black - Load
32k miles, ru
looks great
lv. message

1989 Hond
5 speed, Ta
with Black ir
Power every
Call Steve

1956 Merce
2- door cou
Runs and lo
1 owner, Ch
124k miles

1987 Volvo W

Miss Agatha Bentley, La Jolla, California,
to J. B., c/o The San Diego Sun-Times Telegraph Post,
PLEASE FORWARD

Dear J. B.:

I couldn't help noticing your ad when I was playing in the
newspaper last Sunday. About seven months ago, there was a
family living on our block, and they had a cat named Shasta. I
don't know if it's the same cat, but she stood about 1' 2", was
tortoiseshell-colored, and weighed ten or eleven pounds. I might
add that she also had the most beautiful green eyes specked with
amber I've ever seen. What caught my attention in your ad was
the reference to a blue ping-pong ball. I remember one afternoon some kittens in the neighborhood were playing on the sidewalk with a blue ping-pong ball, and I suddenly noticed this cat,
Shasta, standing across the street watching them intently, with a
strange misty-eyed expression on her face. She seemed utterly
transfixed! She just stood there staring at them for several minutes. But then, all of a sudden, she turned away and ran back
into the house! Anyway, the family she lived with eventually
moved to Miami. Try Miami. Miami is definitely the place to
look.

Yours most sincerely,
Miss Agatha "Smoocher" Bentley

FLORIDA MILK CARTON COMMISSION

◆◆◆◆◆◆◆◆◆◆◆◆◆◆◆◆◆◆◆

September 21st

Dear J. B. White Socks:

Thank you for your recent interest in our program. However, I'm sorry to inform you that it is not our policy to put the pictures of missing cats on milk cartons. If there is any change in this policy, I will certainly notify you.

Sincerely,
Mrs. Lois Tuttle

Madame Maria Abyssinia

Professional Psychic and Private Investigator
Miami Beach, Florida
"It Takes a Cat to Find a Cat"

November 25th

Dear Mr. Socks:

I must say it hasn't been easy but I've been able to track down some information regarding the cat you hired me to find. She is no longer in Miami. I had felt this from the first, but didn't want to say anything until I had confirmed it through more earthly sources. As it turns out, the family she lived with moved to Thailand a short time ago. I shivered to think what kind of chaos awaited a kitty in Thailand; however, I have new information indicating that the family has just left Bangkok and gone to Paris. Try Paris. Paris is definitely the place to look.

Best Wishes,

Madame Maria

P.S. Are you willing now to tell me what this is all about? I sense there is great pain here, the anguish of separation and betrayal. Am I close?

J.B. WHITE SOCKS

Her Excellency, the U.S. Ambassador to France,
United States Embassy, Paris, France

Dear Madame Ambassador:

I have reason to believe that there is an American cat living in Paris named Shasta. It is absolutely essential that I get in touch with her as soon as possible. I have been trying to find her for months now. You are my last hope. Oh, Madame Ambassador, you wouldn't hesitate to help me if you knew what these last months have been like! Before you dismiss me as a dangerous crank, let me tell you our story.

This beautiful cat I've been trying to find—she and I grew up together as kittens. In fact, as far as I know, there was, in the beginning, never a time that we were apart. We weren't brother and sister; we were just raised together in the same home. We played together, we napped together, we ate together. I know it will sound crazy, but in time we grew to think of ourselves as *one cat in two bodies!*

As we matured, our kittenish feelings inevitably changed to a warmer and more romantic attachment. We became lovers—still friends, still inseparable playmates, but now lovers as well, completely and totally joined to one another in spirit and soul! A sofa without her sleeping on it seemed empty indeed! A window bereft of her silhouette was just an empty window staring out upon a meaningless world! We thought we'd be together forever—at least, that's what we *thought.*

Page 2

The young woman we lived with got married—and suddenly our lives changed from bliss to misery. The new husband was tyrannical, insufferable; he hated cats and treated us poorly. A single cat hair on his pants drove him into a rage! The sound of our playing through the house provoked him to threaten us with the streets, the pound, and worse! We were neglected and abused; finally, we were relegated to a small laundry room, where Shasta and I had only each other. Even that didn't satisfy him, though. It became a war of wills; he wouldn't be satisfied with anything less than total victory. He issued an ultimatum: it was him or us.

And there we lived, sharing a small cage together for many long months. Increasingly, it seemed to us as if we'd been born into a cold and senseless world in which we could trust only each other, in which the only warmth and protection was the love we had shared for one another since kittenhood!

At first, the veterinarian was adamant that we had to be adopted as a pair. But as the months wore on, and the food bills mounted, and the prospect of finding a good home for us dimmed, he changed his mind and decided he'd adopt us out *individually* if necessary. We lived in terror from one day to the next! Every time our cage door opened, we didn't know if it was for food, or to change our litter box—or if a hand would unexpectedly reach in and separate us forever! One night, in our deplorable misery, we exchanged locks of fur, knowing that that might be all we had left of one another one day!

Page 3

You will guess the rest. Shasta was adopted out—alone—to a family that later moved to Nashville. There was no warning, no preparation, no chance to save ourselves or say good-bye—one minute her warm body was next to mine, a minute later she was gone. She barely managed a brief, impassioned mew as they swept her from the cage, and out of my life! Months later, I was also adopted—by a young man who eventually abandoned me on the streets to fend for myself.

Since then, I have spent my life, my every waking hour, in search of my beloved Shasta. I will not rest until I find her! Oh, Madame Ambassador, do you know what it means to love someone so desperately, so completely that you think of them not just in terms of companionship or contentment, but in terms of salvation, joy, and life itself? Do you know what it's like to sleep with someone on a bath mat, your bodies intertwined, and suddenly think to yourself: She is more myself than I am! Please help us! My search has brought me to you. The last word I had of Shasta, she was in Paris with a family that had just moved there from Bangkok. Help us be reunited! Help us find each other again in this sad and shocking world! I know you must be very busy, but any information you can give me, any help you can provide, will be greatly, greatly appreciated.

Yours Most Sincerely,
Mr. J. B. White Socks

Paris

Jean-Pierre 'Le Tigre' Alloise to J.B. White Socks

To: J.B. White Socks   From: Jean-Pierre 'Le Tigre' Alloise

Monsieur,

I happened to come across your letter when I was napping yesterday afternoon on top of the Ambassador's desk. It's a good thing Her Excellency is an ardent animal lover—otherwise she certainly would have thrown your very strange letter away immediately. She gets dozens of requests and entreaties like yours every day.

We are certainly very familiar with the cat named Shasta—if it is the same cat named Shasta. She stands about a third of a meter high, weighs approximately four and a half kilograms, and is tortoiseshell in color. I feel compelled to mention—though perhaps this is only the French blood in me—that she also has the most beautiful green eyes specked with amber I have ever seen. C'est une belle chatte! Très magnifique!

How—you may well ask—do I know this cat named Shasta so intimately? Because, she is living here with us in the embassy as I write this! Alas, she is very ill. The American family she lived with was transferred back to the United States, and the poor cat, this exquisite Shasta, was too weak to make the journey home; the Ambassador, out of the kindness of her heart, took her in. This cat is, in fact, in the very room above me at this moment. I am not allowed to see her often (she must rest all day—no visitors or playmates, s'il vous plait), so I have not had the chance to inform her yet of your letter.

Monsieur, if what you wrote is the truth (and if indeed this Shasta is the same Shasta you seek), I urge you to come to Paris immediately. I do not wish to alarm you, but she is quite ill. In the meantime, I will attempt to speak to her myself.

Une cordiale poignée de patte,
    Jean-Pierre Alloise

Jean-Pierre 'Le Tigre' Alloise to J.B. White Socks

To: Mr. J.B. White Socks
From: Jean-Pierre 'Le Tigre' Alloise.

Monsieur

I am following my first letter almost immediately with another. She is indeed the Shasta you seek! Shortly after I finished my previous note to you, I was able to gain access to her sickroom and told her of your letter. She went into a great swoon. Her head tossed terribly from side to side, and she murmured, "J. B. J. B." over and over again as if in a delirium. She asked me if you were here, in Paris, and when I told her no, her entire body seemed to wither in despair. I stayed by her for a time, anxious over her condition and worried that I had aggravated it. She roused herself for a moment and whispered, "The blue ping-pong ball . . .". "What, Madame?" I asked. Her eyes closed and she repeated, in that same strange whisper, "The blue ping-pong ball, the blue ping-pong ball . . ." Then she sank back into a deep catnap.

Oh, Monsieur, please hurry to Paris if you can.

Anxiously,
Le Tigre

J.B. WHITE SOCKS

To: Mr. Oscar Wildcat
From: Mr. J.B. White Socks

My good friend—

I have found her! She is in Paris. I am leaving at once. I don't know how long it will take me to get there, or whether it can even be done. But, if necessary, I will die trying! It doesn't matter anymore—you know I would rather die than be without her now. Not long ago I heard of a cat who stowed away in the freight compartment of an airliner and survived the flight from London to New York! That is what I'm going to try. I'm leaving for the airport as soon as I've sent this. If I don't come back, I leave my kitty bed and my secret pile of chicken bones buried under the hydrangeas to you. Wish me well, dear friend. Farewell.

J.B.

My darling, my darling—

I don't even know whether you'll receive this, or whether you're already on your way. I am dictating this letter to Monsieur Alloise. I have so little strength that I must make this brief.

I am overcome with rapture! I am alive again! Oh J. B., I thought we would never see each other again. When they separated us, I thought I would perish from the grief and the anguish! I had no will to eat, no will to play, no will to live. Even the warm sunshine on my face felt harsh and painful! I thought of you constantly, dreaming that you would come and save me. I searched every kitty face on every street hoping to see you! Every distant meow reminded me of you and I thought: "He has come at last!" They say I am sick now with a virus—but I know I am mortally ill from the loss of you. From the want of see-ing your face, of feeling your tongue against my cheek, the softness of your fur, the sweetness of your gentle paws! Come for me now, my darling! I live only to hear your meow once more! Monsieur Alloise says I must close now because I am getting feverish from dictating this.

I love you more than life itself!

For eternity,
Your Shasta

J. B.—

YOU'LL NEVER MAKE IT! DON'T GO! DON'T BE A FOOL! YOU'RE MAD TO THINK OF STOWING AWAY ON A JETLINER! WAIT UNTIL SHE'S BETTER AND THEN FLY HER BACK OVER HERE. IT'S SENSELESS TO GO TO PARIS NOW! DON'T DO IT, J. B.! I HOPE THIS REACHES YOU IN TIME.

OSCAR

Le Monde

'Stowaway' Cat Survives Jet Trek to Paris

PARIS (OP)—Baggage handlers at Orly Airport were astonished yesterday when, among the luggage and duffel bags, they discovered a stray cat hiding in the cargo hold of a 747 that had recently landed from the United States. The cat was described by airport authorities as "alive but in pretty bad shape."

"It's impossible to know exactly where the animal got on," said AIR PARIS spokeswoman Kathy Solandt. The flight took on luggage in San Francisco, Denver and Chicago before stopping in New York City for the final leg of its 3,600-mile trip to Paris. "It's a miracle the cat survived," Solandt said.

Authorities intended to hold the cat in order to try and locate its owner, if any, in the United States. However, the animal apparently had other ideas. It escaped from captivity shortly after discovery. "It ran off like it had a hot date in Paris," laughed luggage handler Henri Merceau....

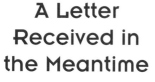

Mr. J.B. White Socks to Shasta

J. B. WHITE SOCKS

My Dearest,

What is there to say between us now that each of us doesn't know already in the depths of our hearts? What is there to say that each of us, in the depths of our isolation, has not thought a hundred times? I am on my way. I may not make it. You must understand that. And you must promise me that if I don't, you will continue to live. You must go on even if I never get to Paris. Live for the memory of me. Live for the knowledge that, if you die, all trace of our love will vanish from the earth. Never forget how much I have loved you, and that when my last breath escapes me, it will mew your name. I am not afraid of death so long as there is the hope that we shall somehow be together in that terrible and mysterious oblivion! If the dead can come back, then I will be with you always: walking by your side through the soft grass in springtime, dancing beside you as you chase a moth through the flowers. And on some warm summer day, if you feel a soft breeze against your whiskers, it will be me, unable and unwilling to leave your side. My beloved, my darling, you are everything to me. We will be together again.

Your J. B.

To: Albert 'Le Leopard' Alloise
From: Jean-Peirre 'Le Tigre' Alloise

Cher Albert—

Greetings once again to my favorite country cousin! I have so much to tell you. You will remember of course the cat I told you about living here at the embassy and the strange letter we received from the States inquiring about her. Well, believe it or not, _he_ arrived. Yes! The tomcat from America—against all odds. He was near death when he turned up on our doorstep. A gentle rain was falling, and the sky was a forbidding shade of gray. He lay at our door—a mere shadow of a cat—wheezing and panting for air. Several of his whiskers were broken off; one eye was swollen shut. He seemed as if he might not last another moment. Meanwhile, _she_ was watching from an upstairs window, as she has every day, every _hour_, since he first wrote. You have never witnessed such a commotion! She—who was once near death herself—started to paw and scratch frantically at the window. If we had not taken him to her at once, she would have come right through the glass, I'm sure. She was like one of those wild animals who, held captive against their will, become driven by an uncontrollable fury to be set free and fling themselves blindly against the walls of their prison. _Her_ prison was anything that separated her from him!

I shall never again in my entire life, _cher cousin_, witness such an event as their reunion. Fearful that he might die, we carried him to her immediately. When he appeared in her room, her magnificent green eyes opened expectantly, and she gazed at him with such an intensity of feeling that I shall always associate that particular shade of green with undying love! I was afraid the power of the moment would be too much for both of them. But finally—silently—with so much force of emotion you could see it all along her body, she moved toward him. And then, after so many years, they touched once more! She leaned over and nuzzled his ear tenderly with her nose. A tremble shook his body, and he seemed to sigh. She began to lick his face tenderly, and—yes, yes, I know cats do not cry, but—a single tear fell from her eyes and landed on his cheek. He stirred, as if reborn! She pushed her forehead into his neck, and his own head lifted back in ecstasy! Each began to lick the other, sweet heads tilting receptively to meet one another's tongues. It reminded me of clouds after a long storm, colliding, coiling together, merging. I discreetly withdrew, and the last I saw of them that first afternoon, they were curled up together in bliss on a pillow by the window, their bodies so intertwined and close it was difficult to tell where one of them ended and the other began!

I am happy to report they are both recovering rapidly now. One would never know that she was the same frail cat who languished here for weeks! They have, I should also tell you, been granted a special dispensation to live out their lives in peace here at the embassy, together, never to be separated again for as long as they live.

Oh, and you remember I told you before how, when she was sick, she murmured several times about "the blue ping-pong ball?" I thought then that she was only delirious. I was wrong. It seems that after they were abandoned at the vet's and were alone together for all those months, some kindly technician at the vet clinic tossed a blue ping-pong ball into their cage. It was the only toy they ever had to play with when they were alone there, and they would spend hours batting it back and forth, inventing new ways to amuse themselves with it. It became their special toy, and the code word for their devotion for each other!

And humans say we are aloof! But then they barely understand themselves—how can we expect them to understand our hearts?

My best wishes to you and your household. Write me soon. Perhaps I shall make it down to the country someday soon (although hay still makes me sneeze). As always, you have a standing invitation to come to Paris—with or without the family—whenever the fancy strikes you.

All my love (which is, after all, what makes the world tolerable),

Le Tigre

Nefertiti and Boo

My dearest, <u>darling</u> Honey-Paws,

I am <u>so</u> sorry about the little fight we had. Is your ear all right? Do you think the tip will ever grow back? I don't know what gets into me sometimes. It's just that you were having so much fun playing with the bottle cap that I wanted to play, too. A little thing like a bottle cap shouldn't come between sweethearts, should it? All day today my tail's been drooping in misery. I don't think I could ever forgive myself if your ear didn't grow back. I adore you madly, wildly, <u>completely</u>. Write me soon, or I will shrivel away from guilt.

Your Siamese Love-Slave

Sweet-Whiskers,

All is forgiven. It's _my_ fault; I shouldn't have gotten so angry with you. I don't care if my ear ever grows back. I'm much more concerned about your eye. Can you see anything through it yet?

He Who Adores You

NEFERTITI TO BOO

Sugar-Tail,

Oh yes, my eye's fine now. It was just a <u>tiny</u>
scratch. Not even worth mentioning.
Are you coming over tonight? I certainly hope
so, my love. I just want to <u>lick</u> you for hours. When
I think of your <u>delicious</u> little chin hairs, I start to feel
like a beast inside—an untamed, uncivilized little
beast!

Your Love-Starved Lioness

Dream-Puss,

I was relieved beyond words that your eye is mended. Of course, I'll be there tonight. After all, you are the most _scrumptious_ little kitty in the world!

By the way, could you remember about the little gray rubber mouse when I come over tonight? I'd like to take it back with me.

Your Himalayan Honey

Love-Buns,

I count the hours 'til tonight. Were any two kitties meant for each other more?!

About the mouse—this is strictly my point of
view, of course, but if you remember correctly, we
found it together in the trash outside Mrs. Stone's
house, and you said I could keep it. (You're such a
generous little tomcat.) However, if you really want it
back, I will of course give it to you. I don't want
anything to come between us ever again.

She Who Longs Impatiently for Your Nuzzles

Darling,

     We did not find it together.
Don't you remember? I found it.
And, as a matter of fact, I would like
it back. That is, of course, if it's
all right with you. I never understood
why you just took possession of it to
begin with.

Your Boo-Bear

Dearest,

I did not "take possession" of it—you said I could have it. And we did find it together. I remember it clearly because it was the same day you couldn't keep your eyes off that hyperactive little calico who lives down the street. (Oh, you have a good memory for some things when you want to.) If you really want the mouse back, I'll give it to you. But I think you could learn to be a little more giving with your toys. Haven't you figured out yet that this is exactly the kind of thing that makes it difficult for me to get as close to you as I'd like?

N.

Please don't start in again. It's my mouse. I found it. I did not say you could keep it—you just took possession of it without consulting me, and then had one of your hysterical howling fits when I tried to take it home. (I still have the scratches from <u>that</u> one.) Just let me have the mouse back, and we'll forget the whole thing.

I'm still looking forward to tonight, my scamper-tongued beauty.

B.

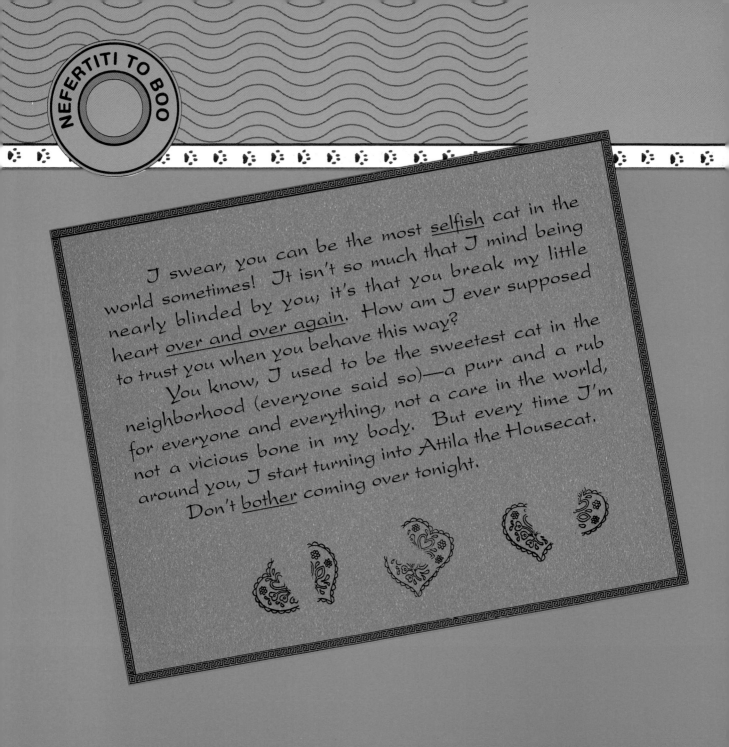

I swear, you can be the most <u>selfish</u> cat in the world sometimes! It isn't so much that I mind being nearly blinded by you; it's that you break my little heart <u>over and over again</u>. How am I ever supposed to trust you when you behave this way?

You know, I used to be the sweetest cat in the neighborhood (everyone said so)—a purr and a rub for everyone and everything, not a care in the world, not a vicious bone in my body. But every time I'm around you, I start turning into Attila the Housecat.

Don't <u>bother</u> coming over tonight.

Here we go again. I swear, beneath all that oily purring about love and trust lies a rat in cat's clothing. It's _you_ who have used _me_, it's _you_ who've shattered _my_ heart (not to mention practically bitten my ear off—and no, it won't grow back— just how stupid are you?). As far as your own (little) heart is concerned, I wouldn't worry too much about it: You can always put the little gray rubber mouse where your heart ought to be.

Oh, I could <u>claw</u> myself for ever having met you! When I think of everything I've had to put up with these last few months—your insufferable whining, not to mention those horrible little smacking noises you make when you eat, and your <u>repulsive</u> habit of drinking out of the toilet—I just want to scream!

Please do not write or contact me in any manner whatsoever again. There is <u>nothing</u> more to say between us. We're finished. I mean it this time.

P.S. I'm returning your rabies vaccination tags, which you forgot to take with you last week. <u>I hope they choke you one day!</u>

I *want* my little gray rubber mouse back. We did *not* find it together—I found it. I did *not* let you keep it—you just snatched it out of my paws and carried it off. Give it back to me! It's *my* mouse. MY mouse!

And as far as bad habits are concerned—didn't anyone ever teach you to keep your nails clipped?! I swear, whenever you walk across the floor and start making that clicking noise—Click, click! Click, click!—I want to fling myself headfirst from the tallest tree!

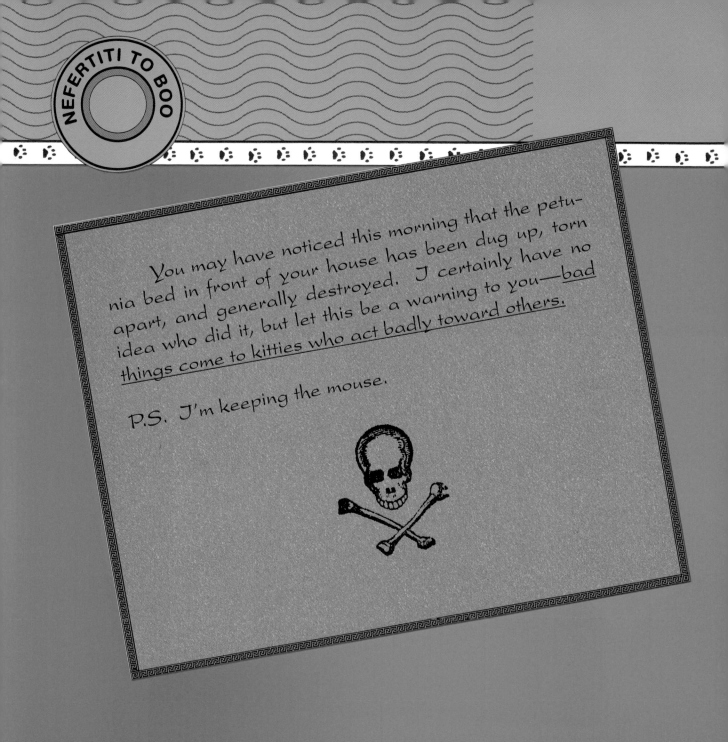

NEFERTITI TO BOO

You may have noticed this morning that the petunia bed in front of your house has been dug up, torn apart, and generally destroyed. I certainly have no idea who did it, but let this be a warning to you—bad things come to kitties who act badly toward others.

P.S. I'm keeping the mouse.

You are just like your mother: self-centered, immoral, aloof—and cross-eyed. And to think that I once wanted you to be the mother of my kittens! There's no chance of that now, you rotten fleabag!

By the way, has anyone ever told you that your paws smell of kitty litter?!

Have a nice life, thistleball.

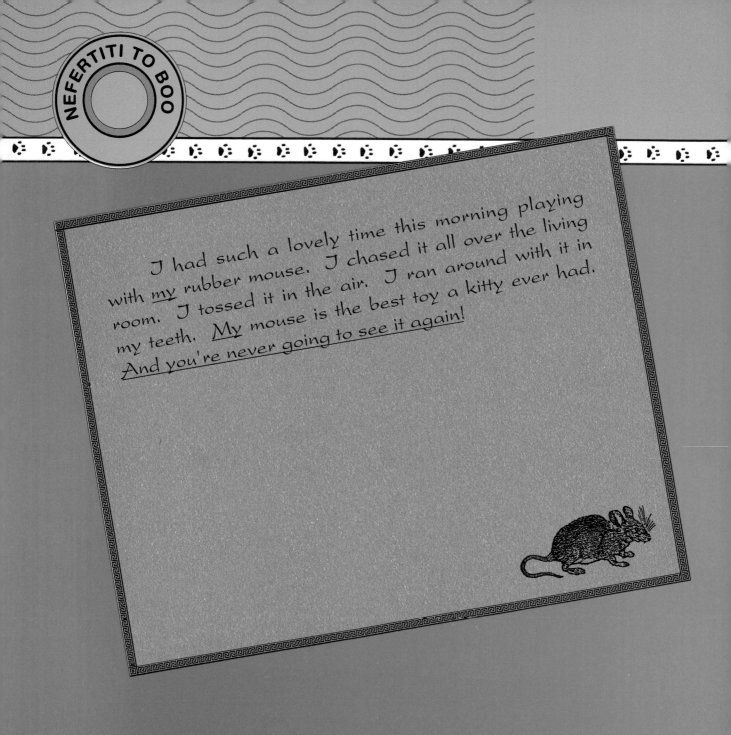

NEFERTITI TO BOO

I had such a lovely time this morning playing with <u>my</u> rubber mouse. I chased it all over the living room. I tossed it in the air. I ran around with it in my teeth. <u>My</u> mouse is the best toy a kitty ever had. <u>And you're never going to see it again!</u>

Furball-sniffer.

BOO TO NEFERTITI

NEFERTITI TO BOO

Bumper-face.

Tuna-breath.

BOO TO NEFERTITI

Pig.

One more letter—just one more letter—and I'm coming over there to scratch your ugly little eyes out!

I want my mouse back!

Coward.

❧ BS ❧

To: Miss Francie Blackthroat
From: Miss Beulah Smallbottom

Dear Francie,

Lovely weather we've been having, isn't it? By the way, was that the Andersons' Siamese I saw rolling down the street yesterday with the Murphys' Himalayan? It certainly looked like them, but there was so much fur flying I couldn't quite see them. My lord, what a ruckus! At one point, I think I actually saw an entire tail come flying out of the turmoil. I thank my lucky stars that I've never been in love. Better to be old and chaste and still have one's kitty-wits intact.

By the way, get ready for winter tomorrow. I hear it's supposed to snow. I do so enjoy lying by the fire during the first snowfall. After all, as my great-aunt Muffin used to say: who needs love when you have a good, working fireplace?

Yours,

Miss Beulah

Mindy
and
D.W.Y.

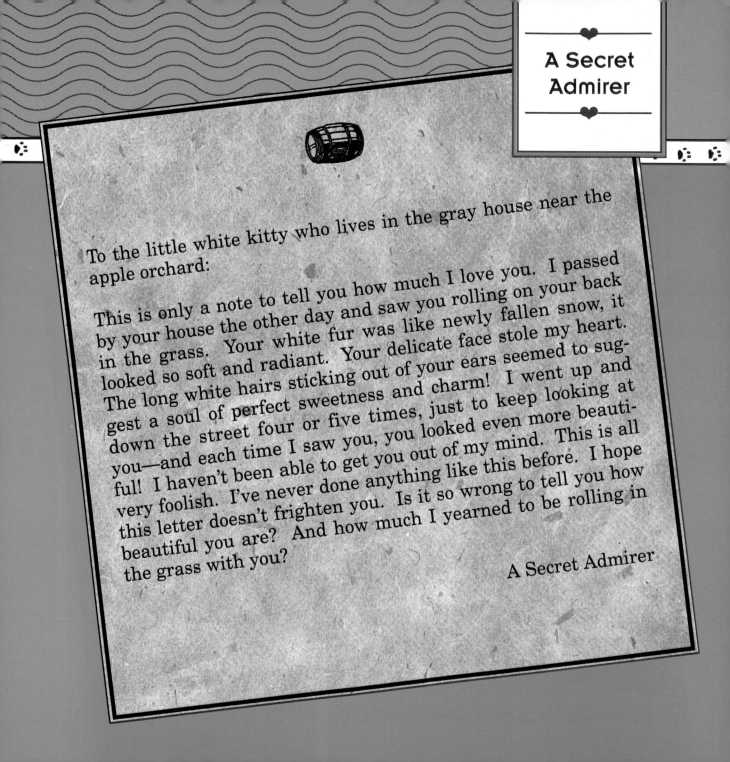

To the little white kitty who lives in the gray house near the apple orchard:

This is only a note to tell you how much I love you. I passed by your house the other day and saw you rolling on your back in the grass. Your white fur was like newly fallen snow, it looked so soft and radiant. Your delicate face stole my heart. The long white hairs sticking out of your ears seemed to suggest a soul of perfect sweetness and charm! I went up and down the street four or five times, just to keep looking at you—and each time I saw you, you looked even more beautiful! I haven't been able to get you out of my mind. This is all very foolish. I've never done anything like this before. I hope this letter doesn't frighten you. Is it so wrong to tell you how beautiful you are? And how much I yearned to be rolling in the grass with you?

A Secret Admirer

Dear Secret Admirer,

Your letter intrigued me. It also made me smile. I'm certain I'm not as beautiful as you make me out to be. As far as the hairs sticking out of my ears are concerned, they have never moved any other cat to such heights of passion before, I'm sure! I usually don't do this sort of thing either, but something in your letter stirred my whiskers. Perhaps we can meet. Won't you tell me more about yourself?

My name, by the way, is
        Mindy

P.S. Don't leave your notes on the big rock by the mailbox. There are raccoons in the neighborhood, and they dearly love to run off with everything. I certainly wouldn't want raccoons reading our letters!

Dear Mindy,

My heart nearly burst when I read your note! I am the happiest creature in the world! Oh beautiful Mindy—for you are beautiful, even if you won't acknowledge it—I hope you won't think I was spying. I saw you again the other evening. I couldn't help myself. You were sitting in the grass again. A small white butterfly fluttered around your head; your ears flickered for a moment, but you never opened your eyes. And in my silliness I thought: "Even the butterflies adore her!"

Your Devoted Admirer

P.S. When you sit in your garden, do you ever think of me?

Dear Devoted,

I can hardly think about you, since I have no idea who you are. I imagine you as very dark, perhaps tiger-striped, handsome maybe, definitely athletic, but with very big ears and with whiskers so long they comically droop at the ends from their own weight! Am I close? Or are you some regal, dainty purebred with a case full of trophies and ribbons at home? Are you a neighborhood cat? Are you an idle flirt? How old are you? I certainly hope you aren't one of those fickle and faithless tomcats who leaves a trail of broken hearts wherever he roams . . .

Darling Mindy, She Who Seduces Butterflies—

No, I don't live in your neighborhood. I wish I did. Then I would sit across the street and drink in the sight of you hour after hour! No, I have no trophies at home (not even a small bowl with my name on it). And no, I am not fickle and faithless. Most of all—there is nothing idle about my feelings toward you!

Do you know I was napping this afternoon, and what finally awakened me wasn't a sound, or the smell of food in the air—it was the sudden thought of your adorable pink nose! And once having thought of your nose, I couldn't get back to sleep.

Do you see how completely you have captured my heart?

Your Enraptured Devotee

Dear Enraptured,

You are a silly thing. What could possibly make my nose so special? I've never known a cat with so much imagination! And while flattering me to distraction, you still manage to evade my questions. Who are you? Where do you come from? What were you doing on my street staring at me if you aren't a neighborhood cat?

Mindy

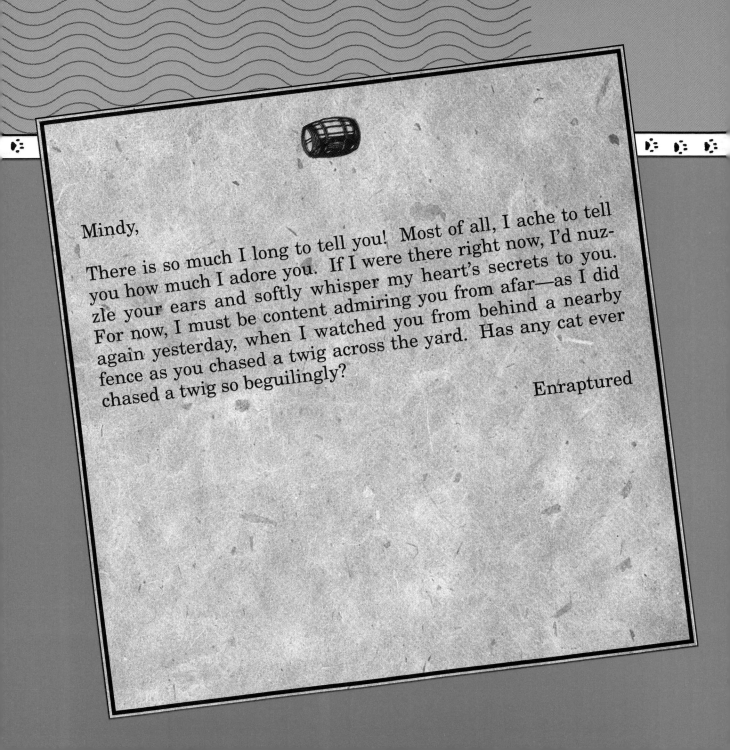

Mindy,

There is so much I long to tell you! Most of all, I ache to tell you how much I adore you. If I were there right now, I'd nuzzle your ears and softly whisper my heart's secrets to you. For now, I must be content admiring you from afar—as I did again yesterday, when I watched you from behind a nearby fence as you chased a twig across the yard. Has any cat ever chased a twig so beguilingly?

Enraptured

Enraptured,

You are mad! But really, I must insist: no more spying on me. If you want to see me again, you must introduce yourself properly. Come to see me next Friday. I'll be in my garden at the usual time.

And I promise, even if I don't like the look of you, I won't swat you—at least, not hard.

Mindy

Disappointment

Dear Admirer,

What happened to you? I was waiting in my garden at the usual time. I was so nervous, my tail seemed to have acquired a will of its own! At one point, I thought the wind had come up, my whiskers were trembling so violently in the evening air. But there was no wind—it was only my heart, pounding.

Why didn't you come? Even after I went inside, I sat in an open window for more than an hour waiting expectantly. Won't you write and tell me what happened? You mustn't tease a lonely kitty's heart.

Your Disappointed Mindy

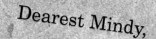

Dearest Mindy,

I ache to have disappointed you! No, I'm not trying to tease you. When the moment finally arrived to come to your garden, I wanted to with all my heart. No one ever wanted anything as much! But I couldn't do it. I couldn't bring myself to meet you.

I suddenly realize now this was a terrible mistake. I never should've written you. Don't ask me to explain. Forgive me. I must leave you. I won't write you again. Tear up my letters and throw them in the road! Forget me! This is all my fault. Farewell, dear Mindy. It's better this way. I still love you. I always will. Even if it must always be from a distance

P.S. You must never forget one thing: you truly are the most beautiful cat in the world. Even a butterfly could see as much . . .

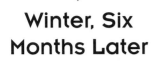

Dear Mindy,

I wonder what you thought when you saw this letter waiting for you on the big rock by the mailbox. Did it shock you? Did it make you sad? A day hasn't gone by since last August that I haven't thought of you. I know it must seem like I behaved badly toward you. One day you'll know why. I never meant to hurt you.

I've been by your house several times. I never see you playing in your garden anymore. I can stand the fact that the grass is all brown this time of year. I don't even mind so much that all the leaves are gone from the trees and that the lilacs and gooseberries are stark and forlorn. But a garden without you in it is a wintry garden indeed!

I know I have no right to intrude into your life again. But would you consider writing me? My world seems flat and plain without you! The other night it snowed, and as I watched the flakes float down through the darkness I thought: "Across town it's snowing outside Mindy's house as well; we have that much in common."

Desolate Without You

Dear Desolate—

Your letter came as a shock to me. How am I supposed to answer you after all these months? You told me to forget you. I tried. It's said that cats can't even remember their names—let alone what they want—from one moment to the next. Oh, if it were only true! In matters of the heart, cats are cursed with long memories! I sometimes wish we were solitary creatures, as everyone says!

I won't scold you. Every cat has his reasons for what he does. But do you know how many times I used to wander alone in my garden, dreaming of someone like you, dreaming that I would never be lonely again? Your first letters were like a cloud of fireflies illuminating the empty darkness of my garden.

I, too, sat in a window the other night and watched the snow fall. But I was thinking of a summer day when I found a letter waiting for me on the big rock by the mailbox, and of how a strange cat who wrote me beautiful letters nearly broke my heart . . .

Write again if you like. I will listen to what you have to say. Beyond that, I can make no promises.

Mindy

My darling Mindy,

Hearing from you again leaves me weak with love, so that even a mouse scurrying just a few feet away seems like only a tiresome distraction and I feel embarrassed to even think of chasing it. What can I say, what can I do, to ease your heart? I'm so ashamed of last summer. I'd rather die than break your heart! You must believe that.

As I sit here, I have only a pawful of fleeting images of you to sustain me. And yet, meager as they are, they are like warm sunshine filling my heart. They are like a spring breeze blowing in through an open window. Just the thought of you makes my tail quiver. I must be a silly fool to believe that no one has ever been more in love than I am right now!

D.W.Y.

All this talk of love. Love in a garden. Love from afar. Love that leaves one weak. But—what happens when I ask you to come visit me again? Another empty evening, with the wind blowing through an empty garden? More disappointment? More trembling whiskers and dashed expectations? You may not mean to tease me, but you are teasing me nonetheless, as surely as if you were to drag a string across my paws and never let me catch it!

Please come to see me. Yes, I think you are charming. Yes, I am delighted by your admiration and attention. But how am I supposed to sustain myself when I still don't even know what you look like.

I will wait for you in my garden next Thursday afternoon.

Mindy,

Please don't ask me to come. Not now. Not yet. I'm not ready. I can't explain. Someday it will be clear. For now, isn't it enough to have found one another? Isn't it enough to share these wonderful thoughts, these feelings, with one another?

D.W.Y.

Dear D.W.Y.—

No, it is not enough. If we can never meet—if we can never touch paws or rub noses or caress each other's whiskers—what's the use of all this?

You see—and I feel I must be forthright here—I'm not like some cats who have a new lover every spring, or who travel all over the city having adventures, or who spend their lives entering beauty contests and having every whisker, every toenail fawned over. I've never had a lover. Excitement for me is when someone leaves the bathroom faucet dripping so I can play in the water, or when a swarm of moths accidentally wanders into the house on a summer night, distracting me from my boredom.

Do you know what it's like to spend one's days unpetted, unpurring, unloved?

No, love is not enough. It requires a purring body next to one, a warm paw touching one's face, a pair of soft loving eyes gazing into mine.

Please, come to see me.

Dear Mindy,

   This is the most anguished decision of my life. Oh Mindy, forgive me! I hope this isn't a terrible mistake. I will come to see you. Next Thursday. In your garden. There is nothing more I can say right now to prepare you. You'll just have to see for yourself . . .

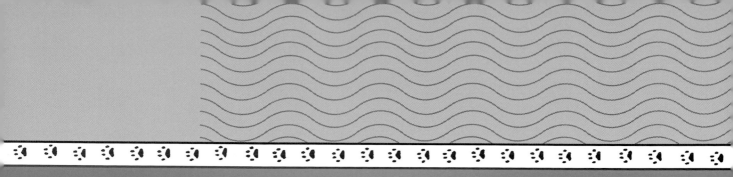
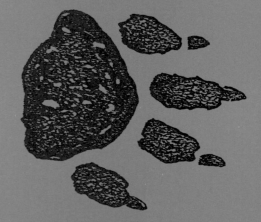

To: Miss Andrea Schwarzo
From: Miss Mindy Softpaw

My darling Andrea,

After a grueling journey, during which we got lost not once but twice, we have finally arrived at our destination, an old abandoned farm in the country. Though really, I like to think of this place as being closer to paradise than either of us had ever dreamed possible! I have never felt happier in my life! Admittedly, it took a little while for the shock to wear off. And really, there was no future for us in the old neighborhood; we both quickly realized that and have no regrets.

You know, it's funny. Now that I really know Beast (I still call him "D.W.Y."—Desolate Without You—as a pet name), now that I can touch him and talk to him and share my secrets with him, I do love him. I know what you must be thinking: It's shameful, it's unnatural, it's a betrayal of all our values! I don't care. Oh Andrea, if you could only see him. He's so beautiful: so strong, so handsome, with his long snout and his big hairy ears. And there is so much of him to rub against! Who would have ever thought I'd fall in love with a dog?! Or that a dog, for that matter, would fall in love with me? Isn't it strange what twists of fate guide cats' lives?

I laugh when I remember that day (was it only four weeks ago?) when he showed up in my garden. I howled and screeched and started hopping sideways! It isn't enough that "D.W.Y." turned out to be a dog—but a Saint Bernard, on top of everything else! I'm sure, incidentally, that he sends you his regards. He's out digging a hole somewhere at the moment. He really is the most wonderful creature I've ever encountered: loyal, loving—he rarely leaves my side.

As far as leaving the neighborhood, I don't see that we had much choice. What kind of life would we have had if we'd stayed there? A life of mockery, laughter, and isolation—of cats snickering behind our backs, and of dogs howling in disbelief as we walked, side by side, down the sidewalk! I needed excitement in my life, but not that much excitement!

Anyway, I hear Beast coming, so I must close. (It looks like he has a rabbit or something in his mouth.) I will write to you again soon. For now, remember me in your prayers. I think of you often.

Your loving friend, Mindy

P.S. You know, I was thinking—there's a charming little poodle two houses down from where I used to live who might be just right for you . . . .

Mabel
and
Grouch

♥

The Big Elm Tree

My dear Mr. Grouch,

Your letter arrived just this morning, and I confess to being somewhat taken aback by it. Really, I think you would be well served to see your vet. A cat your age should be worrying about his bones and his kidneys, not romance! What do you mean, "We've wasted too much time already"? What do you mean, I remind you of "a fresh box of catnip"? Do you have any idea how old I am? I've made a permanent dent in the sofa, I've slept in the same spot there so many times, and it's all I can do to drag myself to the food dish, let alone to a proposed assignation among the lilies in Mrs. Sutter's backyard! My only real devotion these days is to the heating vent in the living room — that and a warm sunny window, when my joints don't ache too much to jump up to it. Please tell me this is all some kind of preposterous joke.

Yours Sincerely,
Miss Mabel Lightfoot

P.S. Did the Clancys' cat, Mirabelle, put you up to this?

DEAREST MABEL,

I <u>HAVE</u> BEEN TO THE VET'S. IN FACT, I PRACTI-
CALLY LIVE THERE THESE DAYS. (I'M <u>AT LEAST</u> AS OLD
AS YOU ARE.) YOU MAY THINK THIS IS ALL A JOKE, BUT I
ASSURE YOU I'M SERIOUS. PERHAPS I SHOULD HAVE
SAID SOMETHING SOONER. BUT—<u>BETTER LATE THAN
NEVER</u>. DO YOU KNOW EXACTLY WHEN I FIRST FELL IN
LOVE WITH YOU? I REMEMBER IT AS IF IT WERE YES-
TERDAY. IT WAS THE DAY BRUTUS THE DOBERMAN
CHASED YOU UP THE BIG ELM TREE IN FRONT OF THE
SIMPSONS' HOUSE. I REMEMBER THERE WERE HUMANS
EVERYWHERE TRYING TO LURE YOU DOWN WITH KITTY
TOYS AND CAT FOOD CANS; THEY EVEN TRIED TO HOIST A
BUCKET UP TO YOU ON THE END OF A LONG POLE—BUT
YOU WOULDN'T HAVE ANY OF IT! THE LAST OF THE SUN-
LIGHT CAUGHT YOUR FACE AS YOU GAZED OUT OVER THE
NEIGHBORHOOD, AND I THOUGHT TO MYSELF THEN:
"<u>WHAT A MAJESTIC, COURAGEOUS KITTY!</u>" THERE
HASN'T BEEN A DAY SINCE THEN THAT I HAVEN'T
THOUGHT TO MYSELF, <u>MABEL LIGHTFOOT IS THE CAT
FOR ME</u>!

Mr. Grouch:

Brutus the Doberman?! He died years ago! Run over by an ice cream truck, if I remember correctly. I was two or three months old when that episode with the big elm tree occurred, and that was almost fourteen years ago. (The tree itself was cut down long ago, a victim of old age. Like the rest of us.) I suppose it's possible that you have truly fancied me all this time. I confess to being even a wee bit flattered that you once thought me courageous and majestic. And if this isn't a joke, I certainly have no desire to hurt your feelings. But why in the world did you wait this long to proclaim yourself?! Why didn't you say something when we were still young enough to do something about it?

Miss Lightfoot

MABEL,

WE <u>CAN</u> DO SOMETHING ABOUT IT. MEET ME AMONG THE LILIES IN MRS. SUTTER'S BACKYARD! TOMORROW! AND <u>DON'T</u> TELL ME ANY MORE ABOUT HOW <u>OLD</u> YOU ARE. NOT ANOTHER WORD ABOUT YOUR ACHING BONES AND YOUR SLUGGISH KIDNEYS AND YOUR FAILING EYESIGHT. I'VE SEEN YOU OUTSIDE ONE OR TWO TIMES IN THE LAST MONTH. I EVEN SAW YOU CHAS-ING A SPIDER ONE AFTERNOON. IF YOU CAN STILL CHASE A SPIDER, YOU <u>CAN</u> MEET ME AMONG THE LILIES!

MR. GROUCH

Dear Grouch,

I must repeat what I said about my age. You may indeed have seen me chase a spider— what you didn't see was that the spider outran me!

My curiosity is aroused. I confess I am lonely for a familiar face. All the old cats have disappeared, one by one, from the neighborhood. Just last week I saw the Morgans lay poor old Fuzzball to rest in the front rose garden. What a wonderful cat he was, always in some kind of trouble! Do you remember the time he fell asleep in the backseat of Mrs. Godfrey's car? Mrs. Godfrey was halfway to the supermarket before Fuzzball suddenly realized where he was and jumped over the seat and into her lap! Her Mercedes careened into Mr. Lovejoy's mailbox, and from that day forward she would never drive anywhere without first taking five minutes to inspect every inch of the inside of her car. We all used to sit on the sidewalk and watch with amusement as she opened the glove compartment to see if Fuzzball had somehow squeezed himself into it. Oh, those were glorious days! Even when you mentioned Brutus the Doberman, it set my mind thinking, and I spent the entire morning remembering how the neighborhood used to be. There were more trees to climb, everyone seemed a little gentler and more thoughtful, even the weather seemed better. More sunshine.

I will try to meet you. If nothing else, perhaps we can talk of old times. But, really, at our age let's not have any more illusions about romance.

Mabel Lightfoot

Dear Grouch,

I am an old fool. Yes, I had some vague inkling of your interest in me all these years; but we're proud creatures, aren't we? And an inkling isn't a certainty, and the difference between the two is a long reach for any cat. Besides, I always thought I was never intended for that kind of happiness. And I haven't missed it, really I haven't — until this moment. Now, after yesterday afternoon, I feel as if I'll never be tired again. My old bones suddenly revere you — as you once revered an impulsive kitten who, because she didn't know any better, stayed stuck up in an elm tree. My paws and my tail and my eyes (such as they are now) could come to adore you as well. Oh Grouch! I thought the mating season was over, permanently, for me; but you've proved me wrong. I feel as if I could love life laughingly again. My dear, dear Grouch! I woke up this morning and felt as if I'd been transported back a dozen years or more. I expected to look out the window and see the old elm tree still there in front of the house, and Brutus the Doberman scouring the bushes for cats and squirrels, and Fuzzball harassing poor Mrs. Godfrey, and the neighborhood full of light and happiness and familiar faces once more. You see, it isn't growing old that I mind so much—it's that everything I once loved has slowly disappeared around me.

Fourteen years?! Why, oh why didn't you speak up sooner? I feel lost, a part of me trembles, and a voice inside says: "A cat's adventures should be over and done with by this age."

By the way, my joints didn't hurt at all today. Did yours?

Mabel

<u>Darling Mabel</u>,
Sweet supple Mabel,

      Yesterday it was fourteen years ago, once again, for <u>both</u> of us. You were the proud, beautiful kitten holding fast to her tree; I was the strong, eager tomcat admiring you from below. Yes, I have loved you for more than a decade. <u>Do you believe me now?</u> I don't know why I didn't say anything sooner. I suppose I've been afraid all these years. And like you, I convinced myself I wasn't meant for that sort of happiness. Or at least I convinced myself it probably wasn't worth having. What <u>silly</u> creatures we are sometimes! <u>At least, we're together now!</u> Yes, yes, I know—we're at an age now where we can't even be sure we'll live to see one more spring, or another first snow. Our kidneys could shut down tomorrow, our hearts could stop any second, our next fur ball could be our last. So what?! Yes—so what?! Life can be cruel. It can also be beautiful—<u>you're proof of that.</u>

Meet me among the lilies again next Tuesday. And we'll keep meeting there as long as we can.

And, if we're lucky, death will never find us there.

Your Grouch

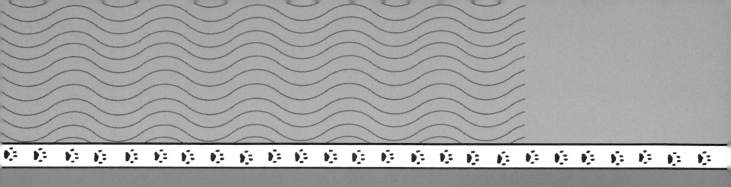

A Note from the Author

♥

All of the characters in this book are based on real animals. There really is a Tonya and a Mr. Peach, though the circumstances of their affection for one another varies somewhat from the book. There really is a Shasta and a J.B. White Socks, though admittedly they didn't wind up in Paris together. To this day, poor Snowball is still trying to capture the attention of Spitfire, who steadfastly refuses to have anything to do with him; the reward for all his wooing is usually a loud screech and a claw across the nose. Spitfire remains, as I portrayed her in the book, a willfully elusive little thing, devoted to the creature comforts of existence.

I live with all of them. The fact that I have thirty housecats causes shock, amazement, and even consternation in some quarters, but I suppose it's a sign of real eccentricity that it seems quite normal to me and I can't understand why more people don't do the same. The root of my love for cats goes back to my childhood (and would probably make a novel in itself), but suffice it to say I grew up a brainy, awkward, and painfully shy individual, and it was a blue-point Siamese named Legolas who drew me out of myself and gave me my first real measure of confidence in dealing with the world. Legolas had been brutally abused as a kitten by her original owners (indeed, when I first got her it seemed unlikely she would survive); she, too, was at first awkward and painfully shy. However, as a pair, we both came out of our shells and ended our respective exiles. She lived to be sixteen, and the day that I had to put her to sleep, when I was twenty-seven, was one of the most suffocating days of my life. Only a fool underestimates the power of the bonds between people and animals.

As I write this there are seven cats asleep on the sofa in my office. One of them is the model for Mindy: a graceful and reticent creature, she is often seized by adoration for my black Labrador and follows him everywhere with a plaintive, hopeful meow. Another is the model for Boo—a wiry, feisty cat whose relationships with the other cats are frequently troubled and full of ambivalence. And then there are the real Tonya and Mr. Peach; they are curled up blissfully together, she with her head on his neck and a stray paw draped over his back. In reality, Tonya didn't die, and there was no unhappy end to their relationship. Although he sometimes gets impatient with her and shrugs her away, and although she occasionally finds him annoying and bats at him, they really did live happily ever after.

—Leigh W. Rutledge